Everything is Welcome

Shravanthi

INDIA · SINGAPORE · MALAYSIA

ISBN
Paperback 979-8-89744-612-4
Hardcase 979-8-89961-623-5

Sparkles of Gratitude

To poet, artist and so much more
Somya Tewari,

for creating a space that held my poetic voice publicly, and got this
ball rolling

This book was reviewed by the wise and soulful writer,
Soumya John,

whose lovely hand painted bookmarks also inspired core
components of our cover design

This gorgeous book cover was designed by the ethereal
Samriddha Roy

Dear Reader

I hope you make these words your own. They may take you on a journey, one akin to mine, and the hope is you know and recognise yourself a little more than yesterday. This book invites your honesty, so I hope it becomes a home for your love, hate, joy, regret, excitement, anger, sadness, simplicity, grief, gratitude and every other part of you that may turn up in your reading.

Use these pages to annotate, doodle, dog ear, journal, paint, collage or maybe write poetic responses of your own, and leave this book creased with traces of your soul.

As the title goes, *Everything is Welcome.*

With love & warmth

– Shravanthi

Contents

1. An Ordinary Life — 13
2. Astronaut — 15
3. Nowhere to go — 16
4. The Window Watcher — 17
5. Hole Love — 19
6. Erupt — 21
7. Cliffs & Cusps — 23
8. Crushed — 25
9. Boiling Rock — 26
10. Pause — 28
11. Orphaned Heart — 32
12. Sunday, I let Grief in — 33
13. This Day — 35
14. Breathing Inheritance — 38
15. The Bravest Voice — 41
16. Find the Forest — 44
17. Wither — 45
18. Hope — 47
19. Let me Grieve — 48
20. Giving — 50
21. Ghosts — 51
22. Mad Sand — 52

Contents

23. You're Okay   54

24. Stupid   56

25. Cringe   58

26. Choose?   59

27. Take Care of Your Heart   60

28. SoulSpeak   63

29. Best Self   65

30. Desolate   67

31. Murmurs   69

32. Bone   71

33. Divine   72

34. Through Fog, Through Hog, Through Maze   73

35. Desire   75

36. Why Must we Save Time?   76

37. Hug Your Prisons   77

38. Nascent   78

39. Love Aujourd'hui   80

40. Bird Cages   82

41. Meeting   83

42. The Journey to Gentle   84

43. Gloom   86

44. Remedy   88

45. Oh! Hello there   90

46. Petticoat Days   93

47. Incidentally   95

48. Love & Age   97

Contents

49. The Other Side   100

50. Last Sighs   104

51. An Old River Dies   107

52. What is it Like?   108

53. Apricity   110

54. The Unknown   111

55. As my Being   113

56. Here   114

An Ordinary Life

Do not fear an ordinary life

Do not throw over it the noose of your disdain

But instead, immerse yourself in it

So much so that you find

The ocean and the cosmos within it

It happened upon me once,

In a most mundane, vulnerable moment

While sitting on the loo doing what one does on loos

The singular realization

"How many souls lived full, successful, enlightened lives

Within the richness of its quiet

And the meditations of its repetitions"

All they did was dedicate themselves to it,

Engulfed their awareness within it

And prized their learnings

As the sacred gifts of this life

Finally, when their time came,

Departed with the peace and grace

Of ones with the universe's secret

They were whole and belonged all along

All the while

In the eyes of performance

They may never even have existed

Astronaut

Amidst the hills, the crickets and the bird cries

The blue skies and fluffy clouds

The long grass and the flat stones

The glass rim-stained sun rays upon the iris

I saw the pillar of us

Crumble to dust, only to be blown away, scattered by the wind.

Our rock bridge trembled in sudden realization that it had no beams

 Fell to a rocky bottom

Your once meeting eyes soon turned away

Focused through the lens

Smiles and hearts were acute angled

And my beating drum knew it before my lips could string the pearls

I was the intrusion to intimacy

The foreigner shut out of a land that chose to be alien

A bubbled-out witness

Staring in through the window of a bellowing hearth on an icy night

An astronaut.

An afterthought.

Nowhere to go

A heart that

Has nowhere to go

Has everywhere to be

The Window Watcher

I realized the design

Of my life

I am a window watcher

A voyeur

A witness

An admirer

A yearner

Of the lives people live

Within their little globes

Their hearts

Their wooden cabins with

A gently crackling hearth

All the while

I'm aloof

On the fringe

I understand

their lives so thoroughly

Their moves

Their trips & falls and stumbles

Their winning rises and victories

Their mundanes and banalities

I know what it is

As the watch-er

Oh, but to be the be-er

The unknowingly, unconcernedly watched

To be the one within

The one callous of gazes upon them

The one so infused with

The vibrance of their living

That there is no other living

To be wishfully distracted by

That is the life I seek

To set down the stare

To lie down upon the grass

Under a warm sun lain bare

Eyes closed, soaking in

Warmth and tingles

Breathing unblemished unenvied air

Staring into the eyes of another beside

Unafraid, unanxious, unbothered

To be restful and unravelled within

Their eyes, their embrace, their touch

Sinking in the pleasure of being

Feeling

Doing

Living

This is what I want.

Hole Love

Why does it feel

Like the waking love

I know for myself

I feel for myself

I give for myself

Isn't ever enough

It is love with holes in it

Hence, as I look for love

I look for love

I know to ask for

I know to sniff,

see and find

The love I know

It is love with holes in it

How does a heart

Come to know

Whole love

A warm, sumptuous love

When a heart

Survived

On crumbs

how does a hole heart

Love with soul in it

Erupt

Anger was the hot coal
I was afraid to hold
Until I realized
I was the Volcano
That homed it

Rage, the lava
that flowed within
Coursed my veins

And the longer I held on
The deeper I dug my nails in skin
Stuffed screams down my throat
bit down on pillows
As tears streamed down

I allowed the boil in my blood
To burn, bleed, peel and blister
The linings that insided me

Only to realize

I needed to erupt & ooze

Effusively

Spit fire & corrode

Lick & Singe

Bequeath gargling flames & molten rage

Upon

Antagonists that inflicted

Thieves that stole

And free my self of bubbling, volatile despair

As I meet the balms of sea & air

I harness my blaze

In gloat & glee

In anger

In anger I breathe

In anger I heal

Cliffs & Cusps

The truth is here

It emerged softly into the room
As if it were there all along
Scattered
Slowly gathering itself into
A globule
Unsteady, fluid, alive

Restless as it paces
Inside my mouth
Trapped behind lips & teeth
While the tongue rebels

As the teeth part
My lips resist
My chest clenches
My body tightens
As the fight to preserve
The status-quo persists

In the knowing silence

Even whispers are lethal

For when breath meets air

Truth will meet reality

And my tongue will write

Change into existence

The known will fade

The weight may drop

The facade lifts

Dense fog descends

As I lose balance

On the edge of the cliff

Trembling

In waiting

To find

Will I cling? To the load

Will I grapple?

Will I fall?

Will I rise?

On the cusp I dance

Alchemy awaits

Crushed

Today,

My heart is

A crumpled paper ball

Streaming blood and tears

Boiling Rock

Are you a boiling rock

A furious father

A raging mother

Cold in the centre

Unmoving

Blistering

Scorching everyone

That comes by you

Evaporating all attempts

To soothe

Otherwise how else

Can people see

All that power

You've craved for

But never had

And when

soft, fresh, tenderness

Is placed in your care

What other way

To be

Than to cook it

all the way through

And leave it shredded

For the world to consume

27

Pause

Constrict. Hold. Pull back.
Breath.

Constrict. Hold. Pull back.
Admonished.
Constrict. Hold. Pull back.
Tears.
Constrict. Hold. Pull back.
Pain.
Constrict. Hold. Pull back.
Voice.
Constrict. Hold. Pull back.
Anger.
Constrict. Hold. Pull back.
Hurt.
Constrict. Hold. Pull back.
Fear.

Constrict. Hold. Pull back.

Thoughts.

Constrict. Hold. Pull back.

Feeling.

Constrict. Hold. Pull back.

Body.

Constrict. Hold. Pull back.

Pleasure.

Constrict. Hold. Pull back.

Protect.

Constrict. Hold. Pull back.

Wall.

Constrict. Hold. Pull back.

Shrink.

Constrict. Hold. Pull back.

Dormant.

Constrict. Hold. Pull back.

Submerge.

Constrict. Hold. Pull back.

Hide.

Constrict. Hold. Pull back.

Witness.

Constrict. Hold. Pull back.

Palpitate.

Constrict. Hold. Pull back.

Remember.

Constrict. Hold. Pull back.

Panic.

Constrict. Hold. Pull back.

Scream.

Constrict. Hold. Pull back.

Whirl.

Constrict. Hold. Pull back.

Constrict. Hold. Pull back.

Constrict. Hold. Pull back.

Constrict. Hold. Pull back.

Tear.

Explode.

Disintegrate.

Break. Shatter. Quake.

Choke.

Fade.

Suffocate.

Matter.

Constrict.

    Constrict.

        Constrict.

            Hold.

                Hold.

                    Hold.

                        Pull...

                            Pause;

                                No.

                                    Constrict. Hold.

                                    Pause;

                                      Breathe...

Orphaned Heart

I come from a long line of

distant eyes and orphaned hearts

The only difference is

I know it

I know my orphaned heart

Can stop searching

For where I once felt charcoal

I now feel a beating soul

For this heart when lost

is found

Swimming,

In silence, in closed eyes

In breath that is sound

But some days she is just an orphaned heart

Waiting for her home ground

Sunday, I let Grief in

I took time today

I took time to let grief in

I took time to cry about my late dog, Lilly

I took time to weep for Watermelons

I took time to witness and feel the disturbance I was denying myself all these days

I took time to feel the warm tears run down my cheeks as I immersed myself in the energy of chaos and grief

I took time to open my eyes and see how truth was being silenced

I took time to see how spineless people in power were

I took time to see how as a lover of truth, how conflicted and afraid I feel to be seen

I took time grieve the loss of innocence

I took time to grieve my history

I took time to see where my terror stemmed from

I took time to see why shame had a hand over my mouth

I took time to observe the circus

I took time to see the blinkers and the blindfolds

I took time to see that oppressors of the world had the same traits of oppressors within my world

I took time to feel my limitations

I took time to see the world as it was right now: absurd, violent, and vomiting suppressed shadows

In the being, in the flowing, in the seeing... there was relief

In the feeling, in the hearting, in the shattering... there was clarity

It is right to be shaken to my core

It is necessary to bear witness

It is essential to feel the shackles

If I must start to look around for liberation & breath

This Day

In these days of pain

There are glimpses of getting better at life

Disappointments are no longer life-threatening

Love is no longer breath-taking

But a search for peace and breath

And in the sadness and grief of budding love lost

My heart cracks, aches and throbs

And no longer shatters into fine scattered mirror dust

That leave me heaving, clawing and clutching to keep together.

In my pain,

I am still intact in chunks

Intact in platonic love, in self, in success,

Intact in keeping myself, me

In the long, arduous trek here

The years journeyed through caves and trenches

Falling through ravines, twisting ankles

Entangled in vines and weeds

Scrawled upon by thorns

And the loss of grip on the slippery slopes of flashbacks

In the delusional snares of nostalgia

There were days

There Are days

Where I am lost,

Wincing and whining

Under the fatigue of old pains and injuries

Yet,

Healing in subtlety and sloth

Healing in hope and the lack

Healing, even in the land of the lost, never arrests

Scabs and scars are my map

Of the crimson rivers that once ran from them

They are the reminders to the I

The Guardians against the they,

Of the layered vaults

Of vulnerabilities and victories

I bear within my depths

The braille upon my body when I lose sight

The oath my being speaks when my voice forgets

The truth I hold when the world falls silent

This day,

In my pain, I am perched on a new peak

In my pain, I have retained love for me

In my pain, I am letting go of thee

Breathing Inheritance

Today was one of those days

Where I laughed and triumphed at work

I returned home

Crashed on the diwan

And then

Wept

Bawled

Crumbled

For hours

I felt myself empty

In buckets and rivers

A reservoir I didn't even know

Was filled by

A quiet, heavy monsoon

I felt like a tea kettle

Holding stale tea

Pour out over a sink

Mulchy herbal leaves

That had been sitting for days

I find myself

vacant

Neutral

Fatigued

Drained

Space

I watch my body

As she sinks into her wisdom

Into sloth

Unclogging blocked plumbing

Flushing a coagulated heart and her vessels

Holding on to sentiments

While the tides of time

Urge the usherance of the new

I draw wonder upon my feminine

All these moons

To now finally feel

Tendrils of connection

To the ancient and eternal

Within all of my big little me

With sight and vision that feels fresh, anew, and evolved

Roots of Understanding

Cellular

An inheritance I never felt before

A womb I am now, in sudden, present to

How interesting...

My body, she is waking up to herself

Her most herself self

Untrapping existence

Fresh

Old existence

Wrapped in muslin

Safe within an ornate carved chest-nut

See, what these waters have found!

Oh! how interesting

The Bravest Voice

The bravest voice she's ever had is the one

that quivered and trembled.

The voice that had tears rolling down her cheeks

and saying it's going to get better

The bravest voice she's ever had is the one

that whispered don't move, stand your ground,

"what's happening to you is wrong

but watch and remember the look of terror behind the strike"

The bravest voice she's ever had is the one

that saw her heart betrayed, broken and stomped on

and chose to say we'll make peace with this someday

The bravest voice she's ever had is the one

that said No

even though the terror threatened to hurt her and did

The bravest voice she's ever had is the one

that chose honesty over being liked

even though they shunned her for her love of truth

The bravest voice she's ever had is the one

that told her to hide and run

when the world chose to abandon her

The bravest voice she's ever had is the one

that told her to protect herself than care for the hurting,

because the hurting were hurting her

The bravest voice she's ever had is the one

that softly asked her to try even when she was afraid

The bravest voice she's ever had is the one

that told her to choose the pain that came with growth

The bravest voice she's ever had is the one

that asked her to rest when her world was burning

The bravest voice she's ever had is the one

that told her she couldn't rescue another

The bravest voice she's ever had is the one

that told her to walk away from love when it came with disrespect

The bravest voice she's ever had is the one

that made space for her flaws and finity

The bravest voice she's ever had is the one

that forgave herself everyday

The bravest voice she's ever had is the one

that told her to ask for help

The bravest voice she's ever had is the one

that told her to apologize when she was wrong

The bravest voice she's ever had is the one

that told her to enjoy love

The bravest voice she's ever had is the one

that asked her to dream unapologetically

The bravest voice she's ever had is the one

that told her to take a chance

The bravest voice she's ever had is the one

that told her to believe in her magic

The bravest voice she's ever had is the one

that told her to choose peace

Find the Forest

More often than not

You need to

let go of the ropes

you were handed

And walk out

let the

sandbags hit the ground

the sets crash

the curtain

Hurry to a descent

And delight in the

Resounding thud

Of your existence

Eyes forward

As your feet

planting one firm foot

In front of the other

Finds its way to

The forest

Wither

I wish to wither

For my leaves to shrivel, dry and fall

For my branches to lay bare

And for my wholeness to droop

To droop under the weight of holding

myself up

To slouch down low and allow the burden to fall

to the ground

For me to protect and reclaim what is mine

I wish for winter to come upon

So I may shelter no one but myself

As I withdraw life back to my roots

And conserve in stillness

Dry the sap that glistens

Balm the wounds that sting

And rest in the quiet comfort the moist soil

offers deep beneath

Safe from feet, and daggers carving names upon

my bark

From hands that pinch at my flowers and yank

at my fruit

From entitled demands of my shroud in times

of harsh blaze

I will give to myself

Breathe into myself

Pour into myself

I will bare my ugliness and

redeem my peace

And in my time

When I am full

Rooted and rich

I will bloom once more

Hope

Hope is allowing the next moment to exist.

So often hope is painted and auditioned as light, and joyous, filled with potential; a vision; a future.

It isn't. At least not when we don't have any of that to give.

Not when there's death
Not when there's loss
Not when there's heartbreak

Hope is allowing

The next inhale
The next exhale

Let me Grieve

Let me reside in my grief

for some time

To savour it

Isn't it here because

I loved

I thrived

I imagined

Things of beauty

Things of joy

Can I not be heartbroken,

rightfully?

Why must I flitter and rush to painfree

When there is richness to be

Picked up

Caressed

Snuggled

And mourned

Mourned that this home may no longer come to be

That our path of love arrests here

Can I not rest here as well,

to look around,

And take in

Our sum

Who I have become

And see,

this is all us together got to be

and soak in the sadness

Mull in the melancholy

Of all the paradises that will never be,

before I let go

to let in differently

Let me kiss the air

bid adieu softly

To this place

Where ifs and wishes once resided

Let me grieve

Giving

Today I gift myself time and the pleasure of not knowing

I lift the boulder off my chest and raise the island off of my head

and allow myself to be suspended in the waters of unknown

I let the waters flush into my mind

and wash away the sand heaps that have gathered

and smoothen the sand shores

to the tabula rasa once more

I lay afloat in peace

as I buoy up to the surface

eyes closed, sun facing, starfished, driftwooded

the warmed blue atmos above

soaking in surrender

I give in

to the waves

to the salty breeze

to the licks of brine and distant keels

all I do is breathe

Ghosts

As I collect deaths in life
friends, family, lovers,
snouts, tails and paws

Ghosts, once horrors
Now, gentle glimmers

How lovely it is to know
I am cloaked with warmth
by loving spirits
even when I feel alone

Hauntings,
Now, welcome pyjama parties

Where I ask
Those soft questions
Those that matter

Are you loved?
Are you joyous?
Are you at peace?

then quiet

and whisper,

If I stay here a little longer, will you wait for me?

Mad Sand

Madness is the sand of acceptance

'I' am the dry sand falling

Through desperate fingers

Of structure, beliefs, and importance

'I' is the sandcastle on the shore

Believing that engulfing waves do not exist

Acceptance is nothing but a mere opinion

An interpretation

It is as if the sand recognises it is sand

It feels useless in the grander scheme of things

But acceptance is useful to the sand

It is not essential, necessary or important

But it is useful

It is useful so sand can now

Learn to be all that sand is

More willingly

So, sand can now be sand

With more knowing of what sand does

When engulfing waves dissolve the castle

The castle may collapse, and the sand disperses

To become the rest of the shore

Until another comes to build another

And so on

Yet, never the same one

Can be built again

You're Okay

It's okay my love

You're learning

The waiting is a hard torment

But you're learning

The testing is nerve wrecking

But you're learning

The quiet is terrifying

But you're learning

The tip toe exploration is arduous

But you're learning

The asking is frightful

But you're learning

The sifting is boggling

But you're learning

Most of all loving yourself through the pain is painful

You're trying

Staying in your cracking chest is twisting

You're trying

Seeing the flurry of your thoughts is tizzying

You're trying

Being with your body and waiting for what it wants is cringing

You're trying

It's okay my love

It's okay

There's so much

There's so much

You're learning

You're trying

You're doing

You're okay

Stupid

I hope to never

Lay upon an innocent heart

The rhetorical whiplash

"Don't be stupid!"

To this day

My grown bones

Quiver and contort

in terror and pain

At the mere memories

Of these slays

That ripped through

My chest

strangled my throat

And thrust my eyes

To the ground in shame

Words that sunk it's

Teeth to the core

Of my heart

In a tone that

minced my soul

My petals lay

scattered on the floor

Wincing

As love and violence

Wore the same face

Cringe

Look around

At all you cringe

In this life.

That feeling.

Brown. wet.

Retching.

Lip curling.

Neck clenching.

Ick of Disgust.

Revel,

In your corset pride

Take your dreams

Let them slide

As you peacock

To the crowds

Your clown hide

Dance and drink

And make bright,

'See how well

I barely tried'.

Choose?

"Choose people who choose you"
A romantic ruse is all I see
 When I have a history
Of discarding me
When I have a dictionary
Holding a hole the size of me
Eyes that look outwardly
At the earth without this flea
When my nerves yearn to sail
Away from this heart's sea
When my stretched arms only know
The distance between leashed "love" and free
When these slouched shoulders
Slope down yet again disappointedly
When my stomach for love
Singed in waiting, filled itself on reverie
Lonely was what I got to be
How do I choose people who choose me
When I learned that love is the one who leaves

Take Care of Your Heart

Take care of your heart

As you would a wounded rescue

She knows not how to be any other way

She only knows what she has been through

Put her in soft bedding

Keep her in dark, calm, quiet

And stay beside her

As she looks around wide-eyed and panicked

And she trembles and fades into a slumber

It will be an agitated one before it eases

The next morning, she will be better rested but she will watch you with caution and keep her distance

She will be this way

The next morning

The next morning

And the next

Until one day

She will come forth

Inch her way to you

You may breathe in joy but make no sudden moves

She knows not how to play

She may wag her tail

And snarl and growl

She is confused but earnest

She is optimistic but terrified

This is all so new

It will take some getting used to

It will take some testing and stretching

Some things may work and others may not

She needs to know what's safe

She needs to know you're safe

She needs to know you'll stay

She needs to meet joy and pleasure

She needs to know what they feel like

It is strange at first

Bursts of energy and unfamiliar happiness can be terrifying after everything

So set a routine

Set a time

With fair warning

Do as you say

She needs to know when to expect joy

And if she knows it

Repetitively enough

Reliably enough

She will let you in

She will trust you enough

To let herself go

To welcome your presence

To enjoy your presence

To enjoy love

To enjoy play

She'll stay

SoulSpeak

In my silence

I happened upon a language

A language I had been speaking for eons

Unknowingly
Unaware

Yet I recognized it
When I met your stare

A language of body, soul and truth

We spoke in moments

In gazes. In touch.

In breath.

In being.

"Will you take me,
with my wounds and scars?"

"You have a home with me,
All I see, your sky and stars"

"And when I cry rivers?"

"I will be the banks
that cradle your quivers"

"And when song and dance brew within?"

"I will croon and flow
as your soul twin"

"And in days of quiet
will you sit with me?"

"This, a most treasured ask
beside you, I will still and be
In all lives
eternally"

Best Self

I hurt for those who are

In search of their best selves

I too was one of those caught in the chase and the chisel

The more I sought my "best"

The more I found my ocean of failings

I found that "best" asked me to chop away parts of myself mercilessly

It asked me to play a pious discerner within

It asked me to choose which of my creations I kill for the spiritual masses

It asked of me to be a hunter of my spirit and the butcher of my soul

I have retired since

Put down my axe

Retired my blades

Retreated to my inner glades

I now hike and dawdle

Within

Stepping and skipping around

Wildflower truths

And what I've come to find

Is that a true space

and a true self

Holds a gentle pace

For the mellow truth

That love

in its most pro found state

is a quiet simple existence

Desolate

This soul is tired

Tired of yearning

Churning and earning

Stretching and longing

Seeking and hoping

For the stream

The rain

The oasis

In the humour of

Deserted sand

Barren land

Vessels of hope

Ring empty

Desires to elope

Aching from a foolish

Intimate imagined promise

Waking from the lie

Forsaking the child

Lungs are ashen

And screams

now muted dust

Where there was once lust

Limbs tremble and collapse

In a finite glitching cadence

And in these eyes

A dull realness

creeps in

This spark

evicted

drained

extinguished.

The heart stops

The head drops

All that is left

Is quiet.

Murmurs

When yearning dies

The heart cries

The throat ties

The body sighs

The dictator is dead

The people said

Who are we now

Without the sour

Bitter thirst

Without our neck craned

To the anarchist's perch

A murmur,

We are free?

We are free?

Untethered are we?

Are we to be or flee?

this Breath is mine?

It is a sign

Untether the line

We are lost

We are free

Bone

71

In the stillness

Of the aftermath

Stripped of my cloaks

of uncracked beauty

Robbed of my robes

Skin bruised and torn

Blood borne

All that is

In silence

I sit and see

Bone. Bare.

Free.

Divine

I am closest

To the divine

In silence

The divine

Is closest to

Me in surrender

Through Fog, Through Hog, Through Maze

Green

Gong

Vibrations

Resonate

They ripple through the cells

The cells bend and rise and fall

As the waves of resonance

Gently let into

A secret - a song - in whisper

I am here

Move with me

Dance to my rhythms

A promise of treasure

A warmth, a glow

River of light

Move and flow

Let me come

And let me go

Green

Gong

Flow

Ripple

With every wave

I leave in you

A grain of me

And in me, a drop of you.

And with some sand

And trust in me

The storms pass unto the sea

As you danced along with me

Now...

Here we are

All the same

All the new

A cell of me

And a river of you

Green

Gong

Dance

Dew

Desire

75

Desire

Is an excited

mother beckoning at

you to stand up on your own

two feet to make your way to her

Why Must we Save Time?

76

Why must We always save time?

Why not take time

Why not give time

Why not spend time

Why not make time

Why not free time

Why not love time

Why not save ourselves in time?

Hug Your Prisons

77

Hug your prisons

As you let them go

For they were once homes

That held your soul

Nascent

Time has whizzed by

I am a nascent discoverer

My eyes are fresh

After cowering for so long

There are days when

The colours are too bright

And my heart is too light

To trust the trudges upon the earth

I often retreat to darkness

To know who I am

When my spirit flutters within

On days when the sun shines

And I find my lilt

Within the whispers of butterflies

I fear I may lift off the ground

Never to return

So once again, I retreat

Into shade

To know myself once more

This time I wrinkle my eyes

And look up at the sun

My hands a soft shield upon my sight

A few rays stream through its gaps

I let only my feet bask

Upon dancing sunspots on the ground

The nascent explorer within me

Feels young and alive to thrive

But then I look at my hands

Lined with time

My fingers traverse

The soft river routes upon my face

Running down my neck

As my eyes frantically search the skies

I am nascent and aged

My heart rested is young and hopeful

Yet my vessel's sails hang weathered

From thunderstorms endured

Under many a waning moon

While I lay dormant

Orienting my wounds and hopes

To fresh starts & north stars

Time left me nascent and behind

Love Aujourd'hui

Aujourd'hui

I look back and see

I have loved

And lost

And loved

And lost

And loved again

I find myself

Sitting with questions

That have changed

From

Who can love me

To

Who can I love

To

How can I love

To

How to be love

And it is here

I find myself

Being the rock

Being the river

Being the sky

Being the bee

Being the mud

Being the tree

Being the love

Being the heal

Bird Cages

I see the prisons that cradled me

And every other soul in me

Pretty bird cages

Dangling for ages

I can't help but look around

These cubby spaces that held dreams

Generations of hopes and gleams

The door is open

For us doves

I look at these cells with confused love

And hold them closer to my breast

As I let their dismay rest

That as I choose the open free

I have to leave and let my blind doves be

Meeting

I tremble

terrified

to meet myself

as much as it is all

I have ever wanted

I will finally

see

this is

All of me.

The Journey to Gentle

The journey to gentle

Is one that's brimming

With destruction and tragedy

Our voices soften

Our bodies wounded, sore

Our once bright vision muted with grief

We walk on the earth that much more gingerly

To do no more harm to our healing selves

With every round of our erosion

We find reflections in all things tender

Soft petals

Baby green shoots

Wee saplings pushing through soil

Hurt trunks dripping sap

Our first instinct is to cup our hands around it protectively

Wince at the intensity of their nascence against the raw, wild, elements

Caress it,

Gaze in admiration

The courage of this tiny existence

Filling us both with warmth and love

A pregnant silence

A sacred exchange

We take our reminder

And journey on

Gloom

Gloom is yet another
Season of bloom
She's a slow flower
Tucked away
On a mountain top
Overlooking a floor of clouds
Nourishing herself
In the alter of solitude
Amidst the crisp billow
Still and shut
As if freezing time himself
Yet
When she does decide
to turn her face up towards
And bare her rare magic
Time awakens
To turn the wheel of fate
The worlds of
mortals and gods
Celebrate
They bow in awe
Break their trance

Thawing their limbs

 in song & dance

After an endless age

Of strife and strive

They cry

The rain of change

has arrived

Remedy

The pitter-patter of rain
the wafting aroma of tea
two sets of four legs
laying beside me

The weeks have been hard
mornings have been blue
getting off the bed, a task
this body lost in fugue

Months have seemed surly
friends have moved away
the work and home drudgery
 there's nothing left to say

It feels alone and empty
clouds are more often grey
or the blue skies too bright
there's a want for all to fade

But then

My face was licked
My nights were cuddled with fur
Two bodies of warmth and love
Restful, with a listening ear

Their wagging tails awaited
not only at the door
but for me to get back to me
patiently, to love life more

And here I am,

the pitter patter of rain
the wafting aroma of tea
two sets of four legs
A soul is remedied

Oh! Hello there

Suddenly, one morning
She said hello!
It's been a while

I hadn't even realised
She had returned home, you know

All I knew was
I was singing again

I cleaned my home
I swabbed my floors
I opened my windows
Dusted the sills
And let the light and air in

The kitchen and stove beckoned me

And I found myself

Touching the produce

Feeling the bumps

Smelling the freshness

Inhaling the sweet ripe

My eyes soaked in the colour

My fingers were coming from

Loving remembrance to the market

I walked back home

Up the stairs

In front of my doorway

Feeling welcomed to my life

I picked up

my Wand

Pens and Paint brushes,

Spatulas and knives

In books and blank pages

Pots and Pans

They both required strokes

Swishes and flicks

Colours and flavours

Care and time

There was a fleeting sense to her

She hadn't made up her mind yet

She hadn't decided to stay or go

All I knew for certain

She was here

For now

Here she was

Creating

Liking

Lighting

Loving

Breathing

Living

Petticoat Days

These are days

When I'm tired of feeling

Tired of wearing

Dense coats of grief and anger

trudging in boots of shame

Tired of their sagging

Frayed lining

Of trying

Summer has arrived

So I hang them out

In the sun

And let must meet air

I lay on the cool grass

Under the shade of

A trusted tree

In my cotton petticoat

And bare feet

Breathe in relief

And rest

Let the world

Hold my heaviness

Someone may need them

For their ongoing winter

Birds and squirrels

may take some threads

For their nests

Let the world

Do with it

as it pleases

I have borne it

Long enough

Incidentally

There is joy in incidental existence

Unimportant, inconsequent, meagre in the narcissistic human story
That cringey cloak of self absorption

But vital to the fabric of existence by just being
So that our most important interactions would be the ones with the trees, the soil, the sun, the sky, the rivers, and the wind
With the earthworms, the fox, a hare, a sun bird, a horse, a bear, a chameleon, a shark, a whale! visiting, good guesting while in their homes

That we continually indulge ourselves in a world of wondrous difference
To soak in the know that we belong to this vibrato of beating hearts

To be licked and lapped with the waves of realisation that we are connected

That we frolic & rejoice in being Lilliputs and Gullivers beside trees, bees, and manatees

That our infantile egos are humbled by the intelligence of land and sea

That we tune into the radio of the universe

That we are awake & engulfed in the sacred humm of all our life ripples

The universal language of presence

That gorgeous, mystical space we recognise from within

The deeper we see the deeper life goes

Infinities within infinities within infinities

Caste and kick aside that dingy cloak

That wasteland of self importance

And awake to the sagas of forevers you live and breathe in

And you will sing

With tears streaming

A heart gushing

A blissful dust particle in existence

Love & Age

I love my relationship with age

I love seeing my body change and morph

How I'm familiar with my everyday

and once in a while when I see my face in pictures

I notice a woman

Oof, A w.o.m.a.n.

who has a few more spots, a line added

and a smile that crinkles her eyes even more than before

Pictures with wide mouthed laughter

and a body suspended in motion

with just a little more freedom than yesterday

Age shows me my journey with healing

Letting go, Letting in & Letting be

Strife, struggle

And my wilful decisions to endure, survive

and then, actively decide to move towards joy,

and then some

The way age dances with me,

is a seductive strip tease of illusion

Layer by layer

Insight to epiphany to enlightenment

It shows me the magic of minimal,

the simplified, the honest,

the transparent,

the negligée of life

Age flirts with me through wisdom

The flirtation with truth,

that despite despair there is the promise of joy

Despite stuckness there is movement

In the depths of darkness

there is hope that is stubborn even in wane

It is only as I grow & glow with age

I learn good things take time

Because I now take time

I let the waves of time gently lap at my feet

as a process of burn & balm

Fine things arrive and become

As do I

It is with age I dance with power

Shine in truth

And breathe in being

That in my anger I am feisty

In my action I am gentle

And in my wisdom I play in gentle feist

I allow my sparkle to flow

To be seen

To be heard, drunk and smelled

To soak and bathe in the light it has thirsted for

With guiltless shameless nudity

Let me be experienced

Let them see me

Let them be touched

Let them revulse or revolve

Let them be afraid or in love

But, I must, Let Them

So I love my relationship with Age

I love my layers of reclamation

I love the emergence of silvers and greys be the antidote of appease

I love the glimmers be the signs of a peace

I love my crevices deepen in my capacity for love and compassion

I love

As I encounter my path to sage

The Other Side

It is only now

I am open to

Seeing

That my parents

Are happy

Happy enough

I suppose

Happy in a way

They've allowed

Themselves to be

Each of their investments

Have given returns

There were of course

Many losses

Plenty of pain

That came with it

Disappointments,

And absence

Anger and ugly fights

Hurt hurled

Slicing silences

Unspoken resentments

Lessons and wisdom

From wounds and burnt fingers

emerged

changed people

The stain of which

Has stayed with me

I find myself mining

For gold in what I know

There must be love

In there

For all of this

To sustain

Right?

Even if it isn't said

Out loud

A lot of the time

I wished it were more

Tender, felt and seen

Conscious, consistent

And frequent

But it is there

In making sure there

were holidays

Favourite dishes made

Massages for back pain

Flowers and handpicked gifts

on birthdays

Thoughtful words in cards

Calling to ask

What to pick up for dinner

Putting up with the dogs

(On the bed!)

Ensuring the right medicines

Were taken

Showing off shopping

Compliments when

they each looked good

before a night out

Attending most celebrations

and funerals together

Putting up with each other's

Weird relatives

And more such sliver glimmers

I look at their lives

And it feels full

Lived and cared for

It balms my breathe

And throws light

On what I couldn't see

There was always

The other side

Last Sighs

I want joy to be my friend

My lover, my companion

And I hear the whisper that says

We are light and flow

Soft and forgiving

A life of gentle living and loving

And our heart hums ripples

And our reverberates and gurgles giggles

through our souls and cells

All out to every single fragment of existence

Breaking forth, breaking through

Dispelling and dissolving

Allowing for space and breath for all

I can have this all

I can be it all

All I have to do

Is let go?

Let go of sadness, grief and melancholy

Let go of anger and anxiety

Let go of my friends, my guardians

That have helped carry the load

Bear my big burdens and heartbreaks

My life so far

my Life so far.

The saddest and happiest thing is we all know it. We all know it is time

And so we all smile sad understanding teary smiles

This was the mission wasn't it?

To arrive here?

At the threshold of these gates

Then why does this feel so sad!?

Because we battled together

Losses and victories and ties

Sifting truth through deception and lies

And applauding and celebrating those momentary highs

And surviving through my several suicides

How can one not see this as love?

The loverest of deepest loves

My testaments to spirit within

Through muscles, ligaments, heart beats, stomachs, lungs and guts

To womb and liver

So many many lovers

Trudging through as kin, held together by the ropes of pain and it's overcome

And now we're here

Over the peak on the other side

Safe on land

Time to remove the bands and boots

Where the weather is warm

And silly grass meets foots

And the breeze is gentle

And the flower dance ever so lilting and sentimental

We have arrived

It is time

Riverines flowing down our tightly creased lids

We embrace, and cling and breathe in all we can

To remember scents and shapes and feelings

And finally, we let go

Last sighs.

Joyfully.

Joyfully.

Joyfully.

An Old River Dies

When an old river dies

There is death all around

A slow ungentle perish

Of every being that shared ground

All that remains

canyons and caves

emptied of spirit

Ghosts of a mighty river

that once flourished

Meanwhile,

Amidst a cloak of silence

On forage grounds hidden away

Is the quiet obscure birth

of a pink rill that lay

In wild unclaimed stone and earth

Nestled in the magic of fae

Sits a promise of fresh fates

A new way

What is it Like?

What is it like

To be a butterfly

In your own garden

Is there shade

And water

For the scorch

Of spring

Are there perky

Pollen perches

For silly indulging

Are there welcome mats

For your caterpillar's

Tired feet

And safe canopies

For its chrysalis sleep

Are the winds bearing

specs of thrive

Excited for your

Flourish to arrive

When the sun sets

Is your garden ablaze

A slow sinking

Sunny days

Imbued in glimmers

A river of hues

From seeds sown

In winter's fugue

And when the night

Saunters in

Does it lull

A serene yin

Who gently blows

A balming breeze

That coddle the

Buds to rest in ease

Apricity

Have you ever stood

under the sun

And find

pathways of warmth permeate

From the top of your scalp

Through your clothes

Along your skin

Enveloping every strand of hair

Over your arms

Hiking up your legs

Baking its way

to the centre of your being

Gradually forming a membrane of light and warmth around you

And eventually through

All your walls

Till you're humbled to

Shut your eyes and feel

The sun find itself in you

And you, my love

In transience

Are one with the sun

The Unknown

The unknown

Is a soft space

Possibility

& Pleasure

a wet clay

Awaiting moist

Wet hands to play

Conscious

Curious

Cheeky

Luring you

With an idea

Only to discover

That knowtions

Are to die

In the dance

Of hand and clay

Fluid in flow

Repetitive

And persistent

Its rivers

carving within an

anonymous form

To be birthed

A miracle

meeting of

Conspiring

Its throbbing

Pulsating

Ripples

Are alive

breathing

In becoming

As my Being

As my being

lies sprawled

sunbathing

in plain truth

basking in surrender

eyes closed

gently baking

I feel my self

rise into a

fluffy, light

sponge cake

buoyant

spongy

simple

with a most

soft nature

that its calm delight

flavours, not tongue

but breath

One that just is

love

In essence

Here

I manifest more days like today

Where the sky is clear blue

The sun is bright

A thread of chill in the breeze

Birds and butterflies flitter and flutter

The city's flowers are pink in bloom

I am up on my balcony

Watching this living picture

While the heart inside is quiet

The soul is cradled

Breath is soft and soaking

And my eyes are kind and grateful

Peace is here.

Breathe

With a hand on your heart

Close your eyes

Breathe

Everything is Welcome

(Journal pages)

Journal Space

....

....

....

....

....

....

....

....

....

....

133

www.ingramcontent.com/pod-product-compliance
Lightning Source LLC
Chambersburg PA
CBHW020547160726
47991CB00002B/619